What's the Issue?

WHAT'S WAR?

By Judy Thorpe

KidHaven PUBLISHING

Published in 2023 by
KidHaven Publishing, an Imprint of Greenhaven Publishing, LLC
2544 Clinton Street
Buffalo, NY 14224

Designer: Deanna Paternostro
Editor: Jennifer Lombardo

Photo credits: Cover (top) Gorodenkoff/Shutterstock.com; cover (bottom), p. 9 (main) Drop of Light/Shutterstock.com; p. 5 Peter Hermes Furian/Shutterstock.com; pp. 7, 11 (bottom), 13 Everett Collection/Shutterstock.com; p. 9 (inset) Uncleroo/Shutterstock.com; p. 11 (top) Arthur Eugene Preston/Shutterstock.com; p. 15 (left) Timon Goertz/Shutterstock.com; p. 15 (right) IanDagnall Computing/Alamy Stock Photo; p. 17 Pictorial Press Ltd/Alamy Stock Photo; p. 19 paparazzza/Shutterstock.com; p. 21 re_bekka/Shutterstock.com.

Cataloging-in-Publication Data

Names: Thorpe, Judy.
Title: What's war? / Judy Thorpe.
Description: Buffalo, New York : KidHaven Publishing, 2023. | Series: What's the issue? | Includes glossary and index.
Identifiers: ISBN 9781534543669 (pbk.) | ISBN 9781534543683 (library bound) | ISBN 9781534543690 (ebook)
Subjects: LCSH: War–Juvenile literature.
Classification: LCC U21.2 T468 2023 | DDC 303.6'25–dc23

Printed in the United States of America

Some of the images in this book illustrate individuals who are models. The depictions do not imply actual situations or events.

CPSIA compliance information: Batch #CW23KH: For further information contact Greenhaven Publishing LLC at 1-844-317-7404.

Please visit our website, www.greenhavenpublishing.com. For a free color catalog of all our high-quality books, call toll free 1-844-317-7404 or fax 1-844-317-7405.

Find us on

CONTENTS

A Long History

Wars have been happening for a very long time. We don't know exactly how long because it's likely ancient people went to war before they started keeping records. In the 1960s, **archaeologists** found a group of bodies buried near the border of what are now the countries of Egypt and Sudan. They called this spot Jebel Sahaba.

From Jebel Sahaba, archaeologists dug up the skeletons of people who had died about 13,000 years ago. They could tell from the marks on some of the bones and from the arrowheads they found there that a lot of these people had been killed by other people.

Facing the Facts

Jebel Sahaba might have the remains of the first war in history, but we don't know that for sure. The first recorded war in history happened in Mesopotamia in 2700 BCE.

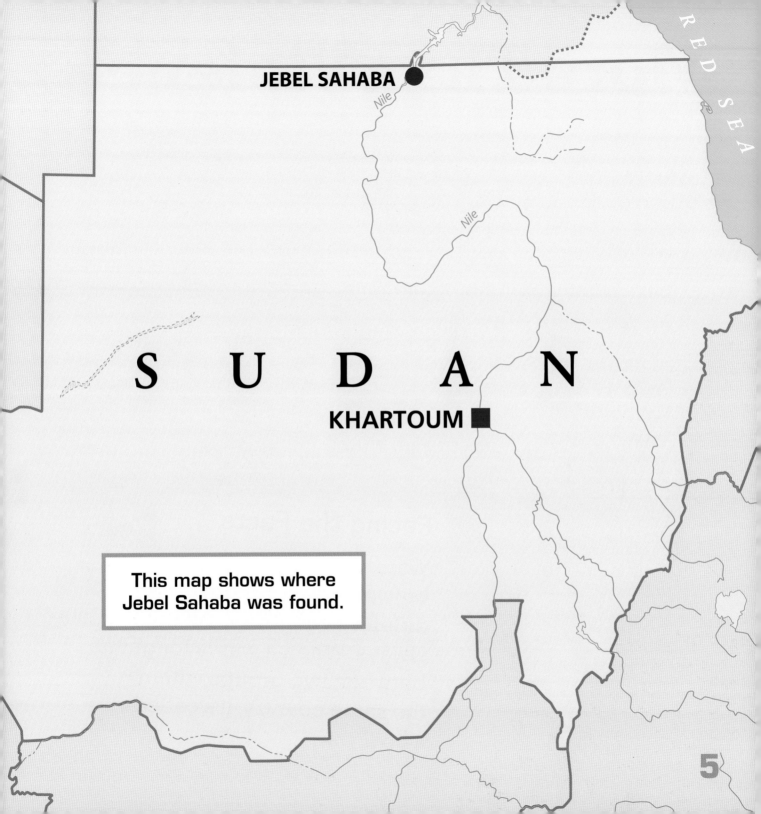

JEBEL SAHABA ●

Nile

Nile

S U D A N

KHARTOUM ■

RED SEA

This map shows where
Jebel Sahaba was found.

More Than Violence

Wars are **violent**, but not all acts of violence are wars. A war is when two groups of people are **organized** to fight each other with weapons for a purpose. There are leaders who tell the fighters what to do and hand out weapons.

If one person hits another over the head and takes something from them, that's not a war because there are only two people involved. If one group of people gets mad at another group and they start punching each other, that's not a war because they don't have weapons and they aren't organized.

Facing the Facts

Wars are often fought between two or more different countries, but not always. When a war is fought between two groups within the same country, it's called a civil war.

In 1770 in Boston, Massachusetts, British soldiers shot into a group of American colonists who were yelling and throwing things at them. Because only one side had weapons, this was a **massacre**, not war.

What's the Purpose?

If war is fighting with a purpose, what is that purpose? It's different for every war. Sometimes it's because one group of people is **prejudiced** against another. Sometimes it's because one group wants something another group has. Often, there's more than one purpose.

Sometimes one of the groups in a war doesn't know the real reason why they're fighting. For example, a leader who wants to take over a nearby country might lie and say it's because the people in that country are a danger to others.

Facing the Facts

Many times, one group will let another group know that it plans to fight. This is called declaring war. The United States has declared war 11 times in its history, but it has fought in more wars than that.

In February 2022, Russia started a war with Ukraine. Many Russian soldiers, such as these two, said later that they'd been lied to about the reason for the war.

Changes in Fighting

Wars can be fought in several different ways. In the past, it was more common for two armies to meet on a battlefield and face each other while shooting guns. As people made more advanced weapons, soldiers could stay farther away from each other. For example, in the early 1900s, armies started using planes to drop bombs on soldiers and **civilians** on the ground.

Another type of fighting that's been used more often since the mid-20th century is called guerrilla warfare. This is when small groups of fighters make organized surprise attacks against a larger army.

Facing the Facts

In the 21st century, many armies use **drones** to fight wars. This keeps many soldiers safe from being shot, but they can still have mental, or mind, problems from being at war.

10

In the American Civil War (1861–1865), soldiers met face to face on a battlefield. The people above are modern Americans who show how this was done. In World War I (1914–1918), soldiers often fought from **trenches** they had built, such as the one shown below.

War Propaganda

Many people don't ever want to see their country fight in a war, so if a leader wants to start one, they need to get their citizens and the army to believe it's for a good reason. To do this, they often use **propaganda**.

Propaganda works by making people feel a certain way instead of thinking. For example, if two countries are at war, they might try to make the other country's people look scary. They might also talk about how brave their own army is. If the propaganda works, it makes people feel more **supportive** of the war.

Facing the Facts

Propaganda isn't just used for war. People use propaganda when they're trying to get elected, when they're trying to sell something, or when they're trying to get someone to convert, or change belief systems.

BUY WAR BONDS

War propaganda like this poster makes citizens want to support their country when it's at war.

13

Problems with War

The biggest problem many citizens have with war is that it hurts a lot of people. Soldiers die because they're fighting each other with weapons. Sometimes they don't die, but they get hurt so badly that they have health problems for the rest of their life. They might lose a body part or have nightmares when they come home.

War also costs a lot of money. Governments have to buy weapons, **ammunition**, food, and clothing for their soldiers. They also have to train the soldiers and move them to where the fighting is.

Facing the Facts

War doesn't just hurt soldiers. Civilians also die in wars or see their homes and the things they own destroyed.

People have held antiwar **protests** for years. The one on the right is from 1967, and the one on the left is from 2022.

Avoiding War

Because of these problems, most governments and their citizens would rather see two countries talk things out than declare war. This is called diplomacy. The leaders of the countries will meet to talk about the things they want and how to get them without going to war. Diplomacy can also be used to end a war that's already being fought.

It often takes several talks before everyone is happy enough with the deal that's being made. Leaders need to meet and talk about what's best for all the citizens who would be affected by the deal.

Facing the Facts

The United Nations (UN) is a group of almost 200 countries that work together to make the world a better place. One of the things it does is try to stop wars by helping countries talk through their problems.

In 2022, French president Emmanuel Macron (right) met with
Russian president Vladimir Putin (left) in Russia.
Macron asked Putin not to invade Ukraine, but Putin did anyway.

When Diplomacy Fails

For diplomacy to work, both groups have to be really trying to come to an agreement that makes everyone happy. If the groups aren't willing to **compromise**, they'll likely go to war instead.

For example, after World War I, Germany started invading, or taking over, nearby countries. No one wanted another war, so some countries, such as Great Britain, tried to compromise by saying Germany could have the countries it had already invaded but no more. This was called appeasement. Germany didn't listen, so World War II (1939–1945) happened anyway.

Facing the Facts

From 1947 to 1991, the United States and Russia were major players in what's called the Cold War. Both sides were angry at each other but were too scared of the other side's weapons to start a real war.

Appeasement allowed Germany to kill millions of people, especially Jewish people. These photos show just some of those people.

How to Help

Giving money is one of the best ways to get involved in helping people affected by war. If you have some extra money, you can give it to an organization, or group, that will use it to help people. Some of these organizations give food and clothes to civilians. Others help them move to safe countries. Still others help civilians who've been hurt.

War is very scary, even when it isn't happening near you. It can be even scarier if you feel like there's nothing you can do about it. One person can't stop a war by themselves, but there are a lot of other things you can do to help.

Facing the Facts

A person who has to leave their country because of war is called a refugee. This is because they are looking for refuge, or safety, in another country.

WHAT CAN **YOU** DO?

Pay attention to the news so you know if countries are going to war.

Talk to a trusted adult about your feelings about war.

If you have some extra money, give it to a group that helps people who've lost their homes because of a war. You can raise money for one of these groups too.

Learn more about why wars start.

If you feel strongly against war, ask a parent or guardian to take you to a protest.

War can make people feel powerless, but there are a lot of ways you can help!

GLOSSARY

ammunition: Objects fired from weapons.

archaeologist: A person who studies past human life and activities as shown by objects left by ancient peoples.

civilian: A person who is not in the military.

compromise: To agree about something as a result of each side changing or giving up some demands.

drone: An aircraft with no people onboard that is guided by remote control.

massacre: The violent and cruel killing of a number of people.

organized: Arranged by a formal group.

prejudiced: Having a feeling of unfair dislike directed against an individual or a group.

propaganda: Ideas, facts, or rumors spread purposely to gain support for a cause or to damage an opposing cause.

protest: An event in which people gather to show disapproval of something.

supportive: Providing help or encouragement to someone or something.

trench: A long, narrow ditch.

violent: Using or likely to use harmful force.

FOR MORE INFORMATION

WEBSITES

BrainPOP: War

www.brainpop.com/socialstudies/culture/war

Learn more about war with the help of characters named Tim and Moby.

Wonderopolis: How Long Have There Been Wars?

wonderopolis.org/wonder/how-long-have-there-been-wars

Read more about the history of war.

BOOKS

LaPierre, Yvette, and Keli Sipperley. *Living Through the Civil War*. Vero Beach, FL: Rourke Educational Media, 2019.

Markovics, Joyce L. *1969 Vietnam War Protest March*. Ann Arbor, MI: Cherry Lake Publishing, 2021.

Taylor, Susan Johnston. *Women in World War II*. New York, NY: Children's Press, 2021.

INDEX